W9-BKA-263

First Facts™

Health Matters

Strep Throat

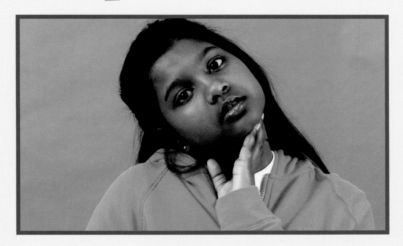

by Jason Glaser

Consultant:
James R. Hubbard, MD
Fellow in the American Academy of Pediatrics
Iowa Medical Society
West Des Moines, Iowa

Capstone
press®

Mankato, Minnesota

First Facts is published by Capstone Press
151 Good Counsel Drive, P.O. Box 669, Mankato, Minnesota 56002.
www.capstonepress.com

Library of Congress Cataloging-in-Publication Data
Glaser, Jason.
    Strep throat / by Jason Glaser.
    p. cm.—(First facts. Health matters)
    Summary: "Describes strep throat, how people get it, and how to treat and prevent it"—
Provided by publisher.
    Includes bibliographical references and index.
    ISBN-13: 978-0-7368-6393-3 (hardcover)
    ISBN-10: 0-7368-6393-1 (hardcover)
    1. Streptococcal infections—Juvenile literature. 2. Throat—Diseases—Juvenile literature.
I. Title. II. Series.
RC116.S84G553 2007
616.9'298—dc22   2006002821

Editorial Credits:

Shari Joffe, editor; Biner Design, designer; Juliette Peters, set designer; Jo Miller, photo researcher;
    Scott Thoms, photo editor

Photo Credits:

Art Directors/John Wender, 9
Capstone Press/Karon Dubke, cover, 1, 4, 8, 15, 19, 21
CDC/Dr. Heinz F. Eichenwald, 7 (inset)
Corbis/Bettmann, 20
Getty Images Inc./Stone/S. Lowry/Univ Ulster, 7 (main)
Index Stock Imagery/Peter Ciresa, 14
Photo Edit Inc./David Young-Wolff, 11; Lon C. Diehl, 10; Michael Newman, 12
Photo Researchers, Inc./Biophoto Associates, 16
Visuals Unlimited/Dr. David M. Phillips, cover (background)

1 2 3 4 5 6 11 10 09 08 07 06

Table of Contents

Signs of Strep Throat

It hurts to swallow, and you've been tired all day. There are red spots on the back of your throat. Your neck hurts when you press on it. You feel hot one second and cold the next. You might even feel sick to your stomach. These are the signs of strep throat.

! Fact!
About one in ten sore throats is caused by strep throat.

What Is Strep Throat?

Strep throat is an illness caused by **bacteria**. Bacteria are tiny germs. The bacteria that causes strep is streptococcus, or strep for short.

Strep throat happens when too much strep grows inside the mouth. The bacteria causes an **infection**. The throat swells and starts to hurt.

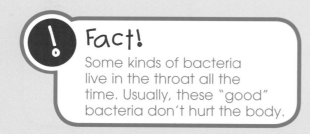

Fact!
Some kinds of bacteria live in the throat all the time. Usually, these "good" bacteria don't hurt the body.

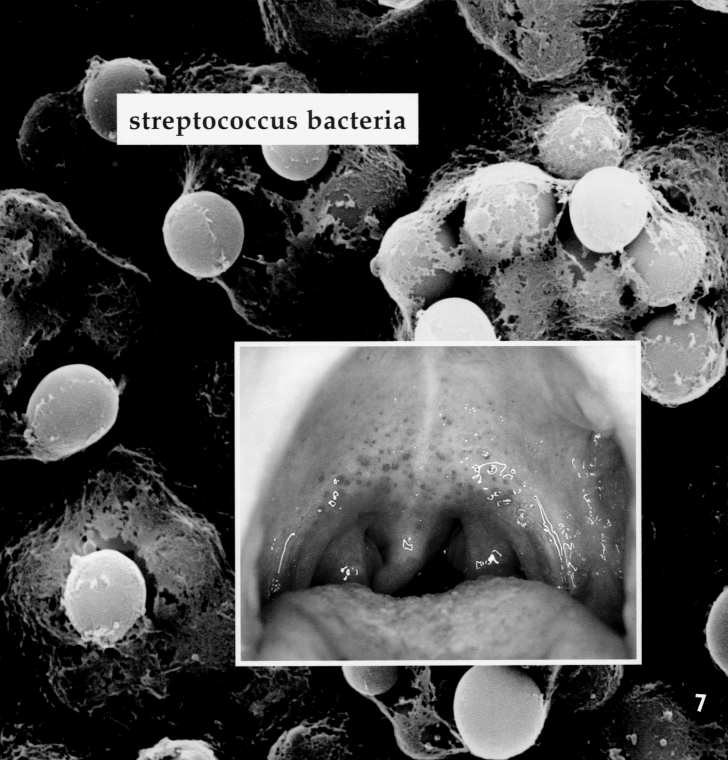

streptococcus bacteria

7

How Do Kids Get It?

Kids get strep throat by being near people who have it. People with strep may sneeze or cough bacteria into the air. Other people may then breathe it in.

People can catch strep by touching things an infected person has handled. Sharing forks, cups, or straws can also spread the bacteria.

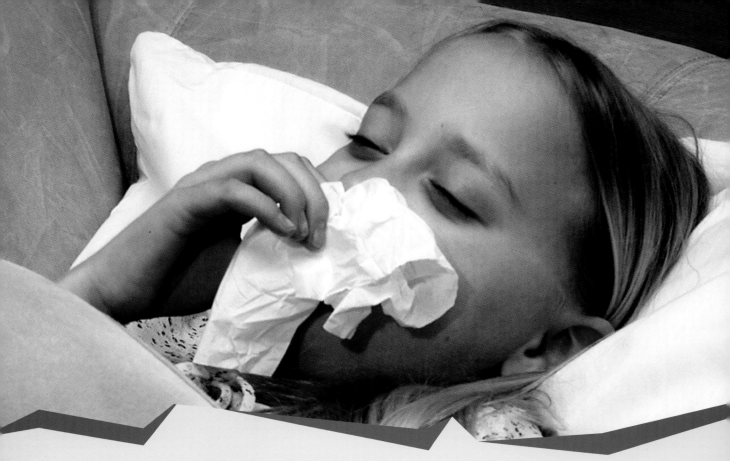

What Else Could It Be?

Most sore throats are not strep throat. **Viruses** such as colds or flu are the major causes of sore throats. **Allergies** or dry air may also bother the throat.

Lots of other things can cause a sore throat. Smoke can make throats hurt. Even yelling too loud can make a person's throat sore.

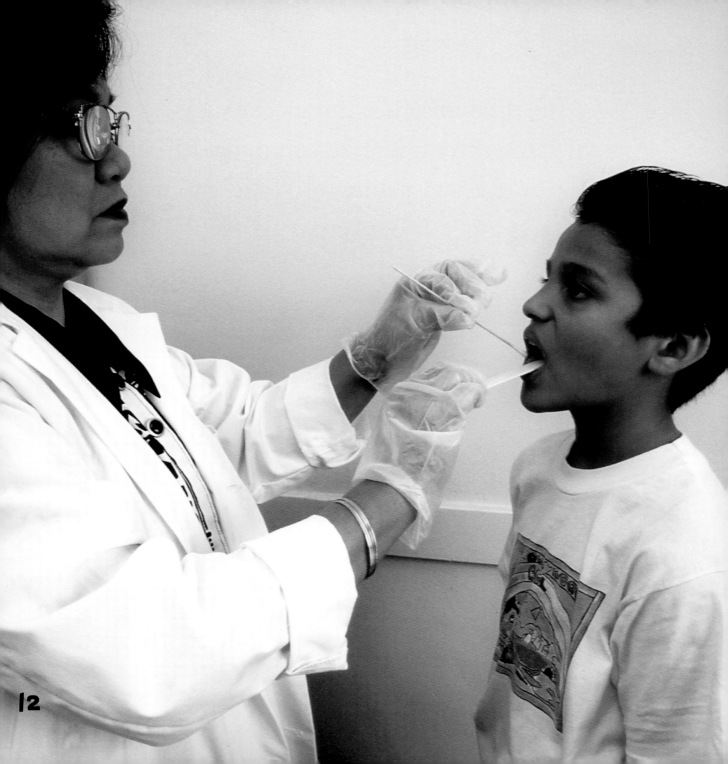

Should Kids See a Doctor?

You should see a doctor if you think you have strep throat. The doctor will swab your throat to collect cells. The cells will be tested to look for strep bacteria. Most doctors use a test that tells in a few minutes if there's strep in your throat.

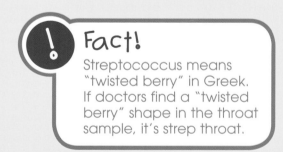

Fact!

Streptococcus means "twisted berry" in Greek. If doctors find a "twisted berry" shape in the throat sample, it's strep throat.

How To Treat Strep Throat

Strep throat is treated with medicine called an **antibiotic**. It is important to take all the medicine at the right time. If you don't, strep throat can come back.

Gargling with salt water can help with throat pain. Sucking on throat drops or ice pops can help too. Adults can give kids medicine for pain or fever.

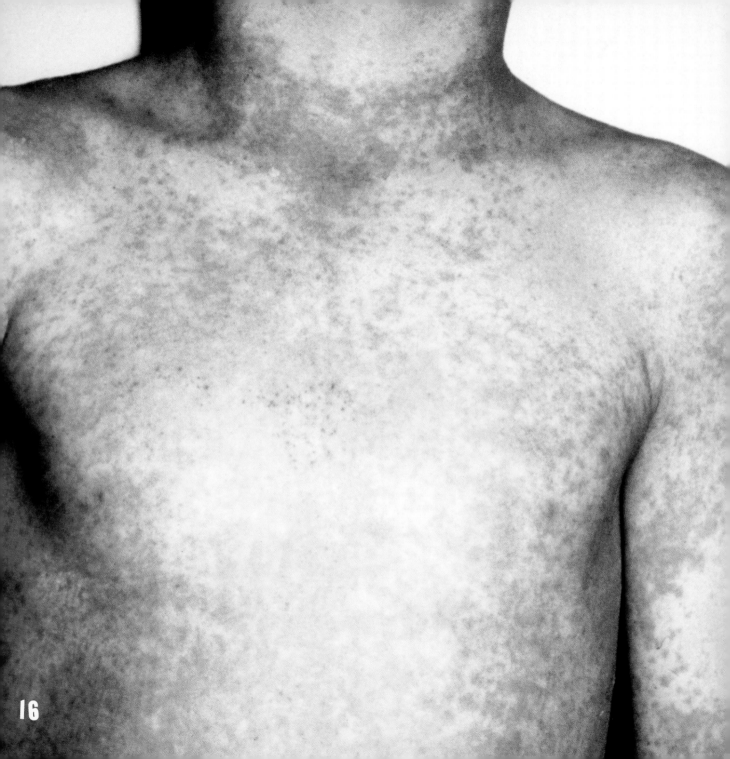

16

If It Gets Worse

Kids who aren't treated for strep throat may get a rash called scarlet fever. Scarlet fever can lead to more serious problems. The body's reaction to strep bacteria may cause damage to the heart, **joints**, or kidneys. That's why it's important to see a doctor if you think you have strep throat.

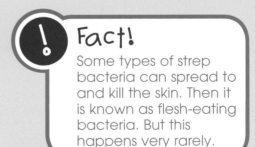

! Fact!
Some types of strep bacteria can spread to and kill the skin. Then it is known as flesh-eating bacteria. But this happens very rarely.

Staying Healthy

You can avoid strep throat by keeping strep bacteria out of your throat. Washing hands in soap and hot water kills bacteria on your hands.

Don't share toothbrushes or anything that is put in the mouth. Try to stay away from people who have strep throat.

Fact!

Signs of strep throat may not appear for many days. You can give strep throat to someone without knowing you have it.

Amazing but True!

Strep throat spread rapidly among soldiers during World War II. Penicillin, the first drug that could kill strep, had been invented a dozen years before. But at first, it could be made only very slowly. Luckily, during World War II, British scientists figured out how to make penicillin quickly. Without large amounts of this drug, tens of thousands of soldiers might have died.

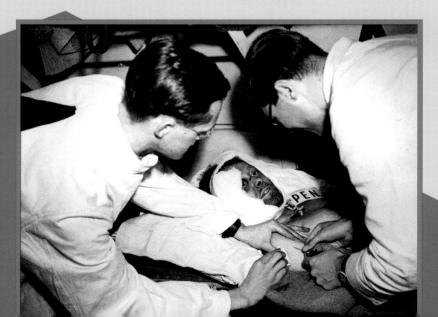

Hands On: The Throat as a Filter

What You Need

glass bowl
tissue
rubber band
spray bottle filled
  with water

colored chalk
chalkboard
2 chalk erasers

What You Do

1. Place the tissue over the top of the glass bowl.
2. Put the rubber band around the top of the bowl to hold the tissue in place.
3. Spray the tissue lightly with water. Don't let the tissue tear.
4. Write on the chalkboard with the chalk.
5. Erase the chalk. Make sure the erasers become very dusty.
6. Hold the erasers over the bowl and bang them together.
7. Watch as the dust settles on and around the bowl.
8. You'll see that the wet tissue keeps most of the chalk dust from getting into the bowl.

The wet tissue works as a filter to keep dust out of the bowl. The dust sticks to the tissue. Your throat is like the wet tissue. It catches dust and germs so they don't get into your lungs. That's why your throat catches bacteria like strep.

21

Glossary

allergies (AL-er-jees)—reactions to things like dogs, cats, and dust

antibiotic (an-ti-bye-OT-ik)—a drug that kills bacteria

bacteria (bak-TEER-ee-uh)—very tiny germs

gargle (GAR-guhl)—to move a liquid around in the back of your throat without swallowing

infection (in-FEK-shun)—an illness caused by germs such as bacteria or viruses

joint (JOINT)—the place where two bones meet

virus (VYE-russ)—a germ that copies itself inside the body's cells

Read More

Glaser, Jason. *Colds.* Health Matters. Mankato, Minn.: Capstone Press, 2006.

Gordon, Melanie Apel. *Let's Talk about When You Have to Have Your Tonsils Out.* The Let's Talk Library. New York: PowerKids Press, 2000.

Laskey, Elizabeth. *Strep Throat.* It's Catching. Chicago: Heinemann Library, 2003.

Internet Sites

FactHound offers a safe, fun way to find Internet sites related to this book. All of the sites on FactHound have been researched by our staff.

Here's how:

1. Visit *www.facthound.com*

2. Choose your grade level.

3. Type in this book ID **0736863931** for age-appropriate sites. You may also browse subjects by clicking on letters, or by clicking on pictures and words.

4. Click on the **Fetch It** button.

FactHound will fetch the best sites for you!

Index